INSights

INSIGHTS

52 INSIGHTS FOR WOMEN WORKING IN CYBERSECURITY

JANE FRANKLAND

The Source Publishing

First published in 2022 by The Source Publishing (https://thesourcepublishing.is)

© Copyright Jane Frankland

All rights reserved. No part of this publication may be reproduced, stored in or introduced into a retrieval system, or transmitted, in any form, or by any means (electronic, mechanical, photocopying, recording or otherwise) without the prior written permission of the publisher.

The right of Jane Frankland to be identified as the author of this work has been asserted by her in accordance with the Copyright, Designs and Patents Act 1988.

This book is sold subject to the condition that it shall not, by way of trade or otherwise, be lent, resold, hired out, or otherwise circulated without the publisher's prior consent in any form of binding or cover other than that in which it is published and without a similar condition being imposed on the subsequent purchaser.

To
MY CHILDREN AND FAMILY
Who inspire me, encourage me, and stand by me when I go after my dreams.

MY COACHES, GUIDES AND MENTORS
Who have steered me and made these insights golden.

MY SUPPORTERS
Who believe in me and cheer me on.

MY DOG
Who sits by my feet patiently waiting for her walks whilst I write.

CONTENTS

	Praise for 52 INSights	xiii
	Connect with me	xx
	Introduction	1
1.	You must build stamina and resilience	5
2.	You will meet adversity	7
3.	You will have to be your own superhero	10
4.	Only you get to call yourself superwoman	12
5.	You must believe in yourself and evidence this	14
6.	You must see confidence differently	17
7.	The workplace is NOT a meritocracy	19

8.	You must become visible	22
9.	You must build influence	25
10.	You must show courage as fortune favours the brave	26
11.	You must forget about balance	27
12.	You will have to make sacrifices	29
13.	You can't do what you want to alone	30
14.	Work smarter, not harder	32
15.	Fail fast, fail forward	34
16.	You are here to change the game	37
17.	Ask directly and with a decision timescale	38
18.	Get out of your head	42
19.	Stop trying to beat the patriarchy	44
20.	Mind the company you keep	46
21.	Your mind is a treasure trove so guard it	47
22.	Do one thing well and be known for it	49
23.	Nothing lasts forever	50

24.	The world is your oyster	51
25.	Comparison is the thief of joy	53
26.	You are power	55
27.	You are not your past	56
28.	Stop buying into the patriarchy's propaganda	58
29.	Practice opposition thinking	61
30.	Cultivate and exude certainty	62
31.	Be flexible; bend like the reed	63
32.	Build strength by recounting your successes	65
33.	Regression is not always a worsening	66
34.	Woman plans, God laughs	67
35.	Lean back as well as in	69
36.	Surrender and free up desire	71
37.	Get good at making decisions	73
38.	No more trash talk	76
39.	Will it and work it	77
40.	If you want to do more, do less	79

41.	Focus on things within your control	81
42.	Grow into forgiveness and let go of emotional hurts	82
43.	You have a voice so use it	85
44.	Don't wait for permission	87
45.	Be grateful and ambitious	89
46.	No one rule fits for women who apologise	91
47.	Pick your battles and handle conflict well	94
48.	Don't become attached, have a Plan B	96
49.	Say no more often	98
50.	Time is just a statement of priority	101
51.	Use masculine and feminine energies	103
52.	Care about being respected more than being liked	106
	Final insight...	109
	About Jane Frankland	111

Resources	113
Work with Jane	114
Sponsor Jane's women in cybersecurity platform, The Source	118
Other books by Jane Frankland	121

PRAISE FOR 52 INSIGHTS

"Jane made every word feel like a personal message to persevere. Jane captures the essence of our struggles with the motivation to overcome them with strength and respect. This book is a go-to for all generations of women. Jane's authenticity shines throughout this book as a beacon of hope for all of us." Dr. Lauren Goodwin

"Jane does it once again – her insights are invaluable and will lift women upwards and onwards. I can't wait to order this book for the women in my network. As the saying goes, 'empowered women empower women,' and that is exactly what Jane is doing, lucky to call her a friend!" Rinki Sethi, VP & CISO, Bill.com and Board Member, ForgeRock

"This is the business equivalent of 'Chicken Soup for the Soul' – everything about this book is thought provoking, insightful and uplifting. Do yourself a

favour and buy a copy for yourself and your friends. You're worth it!" Nicola Whiting, MBE, Co-owner Titania Group

"Any person of all identities will find an insight in this book that resonates and reinforces self-worth and self-love. Great advice and a book worth keeping on hand for a growth mindset and a little pick me up." Dee Deu, CISO

"This is essentially a gold mine packed with so many noteworthy quotes! This mini book offering mentorship and prep talk is not only easy to read and engaging. I love how Jane delivers powerful truths and mindset shifts straight to our ladies; tailored and exactly what our industry needs to hear. Read this now, and get this as a gift for your friends!" Shamane Tan, Sekuro's Chief Growth Officer and Cyber Risk Meetup Founder

"52 Insights distills so much wisdom about life, balance, emotional intelligence and business strategy into such a short volume it should be required reading for every woman in cyber, tech – and actually business as a

whole. I've ordered copies for my whole team; I can't wait to see them benefit from its wisdom as well. This book is great for insights and women at the start of their career but also holds pearls for more experienced women and acts as forgiveness, permission, and empowerment for all of us combating the influence of the patriarchy in our already overburdened and overwhelming post COVID lives. If you don't get at least three aha moments, you haven't read it properly." Jacqui Kernot, Partner EY

"Wonderful enlightenment for those looking to build their personal resilience in the modern-day cybersecurity industry." Helen Rabe, CISO

"This book was like a walk down memory lane for me, as I reflected on my own journey in cybersecurity. There were so many lessons I resonated with, and found myself sometimes between laughter and tears, while I would drift back into the memories of my own experience. It is a must have / must read for all women in our industry, wherever they are in their career. For myself, Jane's wisdom, mixed with decades of insight, served as a phenomenal reminder of the North Star we should all look to. We belong here, in our roles, in this

industry, and the world is safer because of it. Bottom line. Well done my dear friend, and I can't wait to purchase it for all the women in my circle." Kate Kuehn, mama hacker, Board Advisor, and Senior Vice President at vArmour

"The '52 INSights for Women in Cyber' are not only very relevant for anyone working in cyber right now, but pearls of wisdom that should be shared with every girl child, and woman in any sphere of life or career. Jane's insights resonated with me on a deep cellular level and reminded me to tap more into our intuitive life force to which we all – men and women – have access to but sometimes forget how to access." Anna Collard, Founder of Popcorn Training, SVP of Content Strategy and & Evangelist KnowBe4 Africa

"This book contains a great list of insights that will help anyone working in cybersecurity to build confidence, jump on opportunities and step out of their comfort zone. A must-read." Kate O'Flaherty, Journalist and Copywriter

"A thought-provoking and insightful guide for life! This book is packed with more wisdom than most of us will gain in a lifetime. While some of the advice is directed to working women, there is something in here for everyone regardless of gender or stage of life. Not just a must read but a must read often." Karla Reffold, Board Advisor, COO at Orpheus Cyber

"I feel this is a book that everyone must read, not just women. It brought back so many memories and life lessons I gained in my career and wish I had this insightful guidance when I first started my career. Thank you, Jane, for sharing your distilled experience and wisdom. I'm adding this to my 'must have' book collection." Chani Simms – Managing Director Meta Defence Labs, Founder SHe CISO Exec.

"Jane always lifts up those around her, inspiring positive action and change. Her book of insights is no exception. I recommend it to anyone who is looking for guidance, inspiration and motivation. I'm sure anyone who reads it will keep coming back to it when they need a reminder of the way forward or a steer in the right direction." Dr Jessica Barker, Co-founder Cygenta

"This book contains the most phenomenal and game changing advice for women in cybersecurity. It's not a stretch to say that the advice that Jane gives in here has directly contributed to all of my career and personal success. If you follow the clear steps she gives, you'll be walking into your wildest dreams." Fareedah Shaheed, CEO Sekuva, Forbes 30 Under 30 Tech Superhero

"Women make up half of the population, so it's critical that they have a voice and representation in all aspects of society, including cyber. Women bring unique perspectives and insights to the field, which is why it's important to encourage more girls and young women to pursue careers in cyber. If you're a woman looking to enter or further your career in cyber security, then this guide is for you. In it, it explores some of the best ways to succeed in this male-dominated field. So whether you're just starting out or you've been working in cyber security for a while, read on for some invaluable advice."
– Dr Magda Chelly, CISO, Managing Director and Co-Founder, Responsible Cyber

PRAISE FOR 52 INSIGHTS | XIX

CONNECT WITH ME

Free Resources

You can download 52 empowering quotes to supplement this book at https://bit.ly/INSightsResources

Connect with me on:

Website: https://jane-frankland.com
LinkedIn: https://linkedin.com/in/janefrankland
Twitter: https://twitter.com/janefrankland

52 INSIGHTS FOR WOMEN WORKING IN CYBERSECURITY

A fast 45-minute read for busy professionals.

Read me first!

Thanks for choosing this book or for gifting it to a friend, colleague or your team. It's one of a series of books and can be used alongside my new planner. I'm excited to get this to you. Chances are, you identify as a woman, you're working in cybersecurity (like me) and you're looking for some guidance. Maybe you're just starting out, are mid-level, or a seasoned pro. You could be working for a consultancy or in industry, academia, a non-profit, or institution. Perhaps you're running your own business as an entrepreneur. Whatever the case, you've got questions, are short on time and have taken action (by reading this book) to have them answered.

This little book has been created to give you the answers and shortcuts you need—fast. It's a curation of my top insights and golden nuggets of wisdom that I've gathered along my way as a mother, female tech entrepreneur, and executive working in a male dominated industry, cybersecurity. These are the things I would have loved to have known earlier in my career. Things that would have made my life easier and perhaps my impact greater.

I'm hoping they'll make a difference to you and that the 52 insights I've included will inspire, empower, and enable you to thrive not just in a male dominated industry but, in the world, at large. Whilst I've written these insights for women, any gender—or anyone between or beyond gender—is welcome to read them. Many are simply useful insights for human beings.

You can flip through this book and read the insights in chronological order. You can also just stop at any page that catches your attention. I've been as concise as I can be with each insight, however, if you want more details then you'll have to wait for my next book. It's coming soon and you can sign up for it on the waitlist here https://bit.ly/new-book-waitlist.

I hope you enjoy this book. Let me know what you think and what's the most powerful insight for you. Pop me a message at insights@jane-frankland.com

1.

YOU MUST BUILD STAMINA AND RESILIENCE

No woman is ever going to tell you that it's going to be easy to work in a male dominated environment like cybersecurity. Most of the time you'll be judged harshly due to the everyday discrimination, resentment, and immense competition for limited opportunities. Sometimes you'll feel like you're going backwards or stagnating. Other times you'll be dealt low blows and feel like you've got no fight left in you. If that's the case, know this. Sometimes you've got to get knocked down lower than you've ever been in order to stand up taller than you ever were. So, if or when this happens, you can either let it define you, destroy you or strengthen you. If you've been knocked to your knees, know that you can always get back up. And, when you do, you can be stronger, more compassionate, and more valuable than ever before.

2.

YOU WILL MEET ADVERSITY

Life will test you and when it deals you a blow it's easy to play the victim. Don't fall into that trap. It will lead you to the drama triangle[1] – which is where misery lives and where you'll be stuck playing out the role of victim, perpetrator and rescuer plus attracting people like this into your life as well. By all means get angry and release your feminine rage if someone or something has violated your boundaries, threatened your safety, or the existence you've carefully cultivated for yourself. Anger serves a purpose, and righteous anger can be channeled to solve problems mindfully. It lets others know that you're not a pushover, which is important because often women get what they're willing to tolerate. Understand too that opportunity

---

1. https://en.wikipedia.org/wiki/Karpman_drama_triangle

often comes disguised as adversity, so look for the hidden messages in the opportunity you've just received and greet it with an open mind.

When you get back up you can be stronger, more compassionate, and more valuable than ever before.

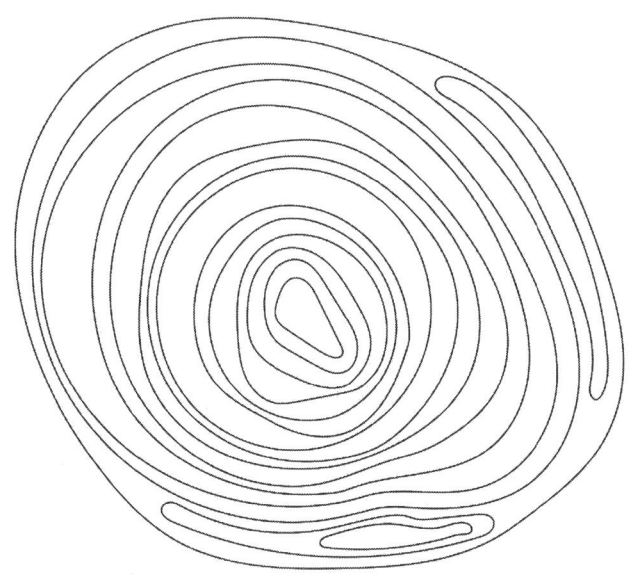

3.

YOU WILL HAVE TO BE YOUR OWN SUPERHERO

Many women have been brought up on a lie: that they're not enough and need saving, often by a man. So please understand this. No one is coming to save you. The sooner you realise this, stick your big girl pants on, and become your own superhero the better. If others aren't there to help you, don't judge them. This will just slow you down and waste your energy. Instead, love these people for who they are and where they are on their journey. Ask yourself what you need, what words you need to hear, and what you'd say to your best friend if you saw her (or him) going through what you're experiencing. Or think of someone you really admire, love, or care for, and ask yourself, what would they say to you if they witnessed you struggling? This is called leveraging the power of objectivity and according to researchers at the University of Waterloo in Canada and the University of Michigan in the USA when you become objective and take a third party's stance to make a decision, you tend to think from multiple perspectives and multiple outcomes, which results in much better decision making.[1] So, experiment with these techniques. And when you get rejected – and you will, as it's part of life's course – know that rejection is protection, and something better is on its way.

---

1. https://www.businessinsider.com/study-says-talking-yourself-in-third-person-make-you-wiser-2019-8?r=US&IR=T

4.

ONLY YOU GET TO CALL YOURSELF SUPERWOMAN

Being called a superwoman is a label no woman should wear. The pressure of perfection for women is already too high. All the superwoman label does is promote the false belief that you have to have special powers in order to achieve anything or be remarkable. It doesn't break down stereotypes, either. That said, there are always going to be times when *you* can't quite believe you've pulled something off. So, when this happens give yourself a pat on the back and be proud. But don't let anyone else call you superwoman except yourself.

Get resourceful.
Find the time.
Find the money.
Find the way.

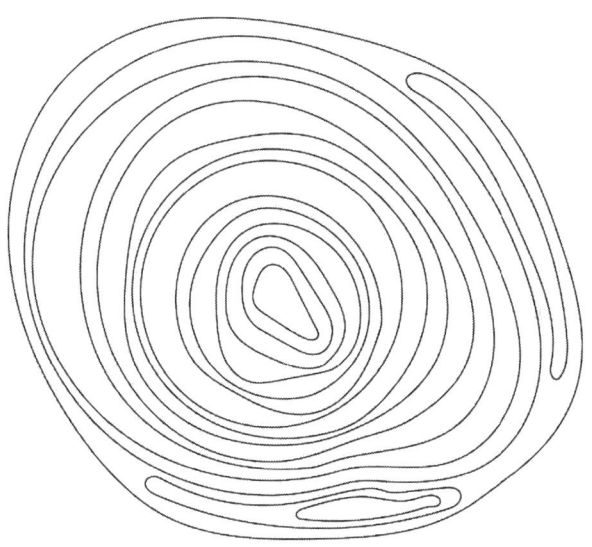

5.

YOU MUST BELIEVE IN YOURSELF AND EVIDENCE THIS

You can't expect anyone to believe in you and take a chance on you unless you believe in yourself. So, take a good look at your life. Get clear on where you are now, where you want to be, what skills you need and are lacking, and build a plan. Invest and bet on yourself. Prioritise your personal development as well as your emotional, spiritual, and physical health. Don't let excuses get in the way of this. Amateurs do that. Find the time. Find the money. Find a way.

It pays off and that's why the well-known American entrepreneur, author and motivational speaker, Jim Rohn once said, *"your level of success will rarely exceed your level of personal development."* So, with his wisdom and mine, please don't wait for someone else to make the investment in you happen. Or, give you permission. Promise me, no more waiting. If you're nervous or not sure about what to do, take a small step forward and in no time you'll find yourself taking another and another. Know that small, consistent steps – otherwise known as incremental gains lead to quantum leaps and massive transformation.

Know also that when you work on strengthening your inner belief, which is your core, you signal to yourself and to others that you're worth investing in and it's a total game changer. Not only will you level-up, but your energy will change, and everyone else will feel it. This is important because most of the time you're using language to communicate your worth and whilst change begins in language it has its limits. But it's your energy that attracts all things to you. Even on camera, remotely, people feel it.

But don't expect results overnight. They take time. You may work in tech, but you are not a machine. So, be patient and kind to yourself. Know that at each new phase of your life, you're somewhere you've never been before, and you're exactly where you're meant to be at this given time. Everything happens in accordance with divine timing. Have faith and trust that you have the skills, talents, and abilities to face all that lies ahead of you. Know there are no bad decisions or wrong turns. All paths will lead you to where you're meant to be. Some might get you there faster than others or take longer, and that's ok. Know that you're safe, protected and your best will always be good enough when it matters. Promise yourself you'll give 100%, so you can look yourself in the mirror and say, *"I tried my best"* and never let someone else's insecurity force you to play small. Don't dim your light for them. Own your greatness. Lead the way.

6.

YOU MUST SEE CONFIDENCE DIFFERENTLY

Evidence shows that women are less self-assured than men and that to succeed, confidence matters as much as competence.[1] As confidence is just about assessing risk and taking action on it, the next time you need to be confident reframe any fear you have as excitement. There is very little physiological difference between the two. Fear activates the hypothalamus, a small area of the brain, in the same way as excitement, and when it's predictable it activates the brain's reward centre as well.[2] So, use fear as fuel to propel you forward.

---

1. https://www.theatlantic.com/magazine/archive/2014/05/the-confidence-gap/359815/
2. https://www.psychologytoday.com/us/blog/prefrontal-nudity/201410/predictable-fear

Use author and motivational speaker Mel Robbin's 5 second rule: Whenever you're asked to do something that might take you out of your comfort zone, for example speaking at an event, presenting, leading, or stepping into a new role, all you have to do is take a deep breath, count backwards in your head (5-4-3-2-1) and then say, *"thank you for giving me this opportunity."* Alternatively, look at your fear with a coach, counsellor or therapist and ascertain whether the fear has real reference points, has been inherited (due to culture) or has been made up. More often than not untruths enter our mind accidentally.

7.

THE WORKPLACE IS NOT A MERITOCRACY

The workplace is not a level playing field for women. Meritocracy is a myth. However, many people genuinely believe it is a reality, especially men in tech companies. Ironically, big data proves its disfunction – that believing in meritocracy makes people more selfish, less self-critical, and more prone to introduce bias and behave in a discriminatory way. The same goes for organisations which present themselves as meritocratic. There, managers favour men over equally qualified women. So, understand this: you can't apply the same tactics that men use to advance their careers. It doesn't work for women. In fact, when women do this, they do worse. You need to work on visibility, gaining recognition from your manager and getting access to powerful people. It's the number one thing a woman can do to advance her career.

Rejection is protection. Better is on its way.

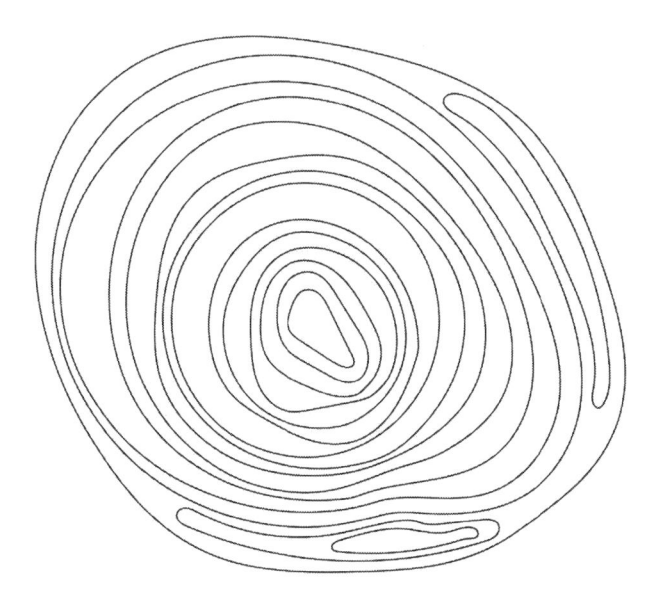

8.

YOU MUST BECOME VISIBLE

There are two types of work, visible work and invisible work, and only one delivers a better return on your investment. It's visible work and the reason why is because your value decreases based upon someone's inability to see your worth. Whilst some people might say it won't if you work for a good leader or that you won't be defined by your productivity, don't be fooled. In the workplace this is not the case. Everyone is accountable and dispensable. Becoming visible through personal branding efforts such as writing, speaking, or setting up social initiatives, is how you demonstrate your value and thought leadership in the workplace. You don't achieve these things with qualifications and certifications. They fulfill another purpose.

You see, perception is reality and there are many more stakeholders you need to influence beyond your leader. Today, right now, your line of work is topical and it's exposing you to new areas in an organisation. Stakeholders need to know about you and feel comfortable talking to you. Raising your visibility and developing a voice enables you to be taken seriously and sell faster throughout the ecosystem. It enables you to get recognition and be financially rewarded. In your case, as a woman, it increases your chances of attaining fair pay, promotions, and access to exciting projects within the organisation or outside of it. Think of raising your visibility as a risk mitigation strategy.

Visibility keeps you current in your chosen field, too. It opens doors for you and creates a lasting impression on others. When you build a personal brand to support your visibility efforts, it works just like any successful brand does – it self-promotes, stimulates a unique experience, and breathes loyalty and consistency into the quality of the service it offers. If you're a hiring manager or leading a team, it facilitates awareness and helps you attract top talent. And, if you're responsible for developing business, it attracts your ideal buyer.

Visibility also helps with bias and as you know women are subjected to a phenomenal amount of bias in the workplace. Stereotype threat is well known but the one I want you to know about is The Pygmalion effect. This is a psychological phenomenon wherein high expectations lead to improved performance in a given area. Studies have shown that top students or employees don't necessarily do better because of their natural ability. Rather it's because they get more attention or receive better opportunities and working conditions.

So, if you're not seen you won't get nearly as many opportunities as you could if you were more visible. You see, what we achieve, how we think, how we act, and how we perceive our capabilities can be influenced by the expectations of those around us. So as a woman, you can use this knowledge to keep you playing small or to rise! You choose.

9.

YOU MUST BUILD INFLUENCE

As success hinges on the ability to influence people to achieve common goals and purposes it's vital you build this new power of competence if you're to achieve what you're capable of. This means building trust through personal effectiveness and an approach that pulls and attracts. Additionally, moving away from how personal power was set in the past, which was based on a hierarchy system that used job titles plus a command-and-control, push and force approach.

Building influence also puts you inside an inner circle where you'll be one of a few who'll be getting access to many opportunities.

10.

YOU MUST SHOW COURAGE AS FORTUNE FAVOURS THE BRAVE

Get used to stepping outside of your comfort zone. It's where the magic happens. Sometimes this will mean pushing yourself forward for promotion, nominating yourself for an award, seizing an opportunity, speaking up or at an event, leading a team, standing up for what you believe to be right, or even retreating, surrendering, and going with the flow. When your impostor syndrome shows up, because it's going to try and keep you safe, manage it. It's not evidence of your inability.

11.

YOU MUST FORGET ABOUT BALANCE

In order to evolve you need movement and that doesn't come from something that's stationary, like balance. In fact, balance is a myth. Chasing it, therefore, is like believing in flying pigs, fairies, or unicorns. Remember that you are a life force so show curiosity or passion instead of balance. Trust your gut and your intuition. Do what you love and stay available for miracles because they are everywhere.

Your best will be good enough when it matters.

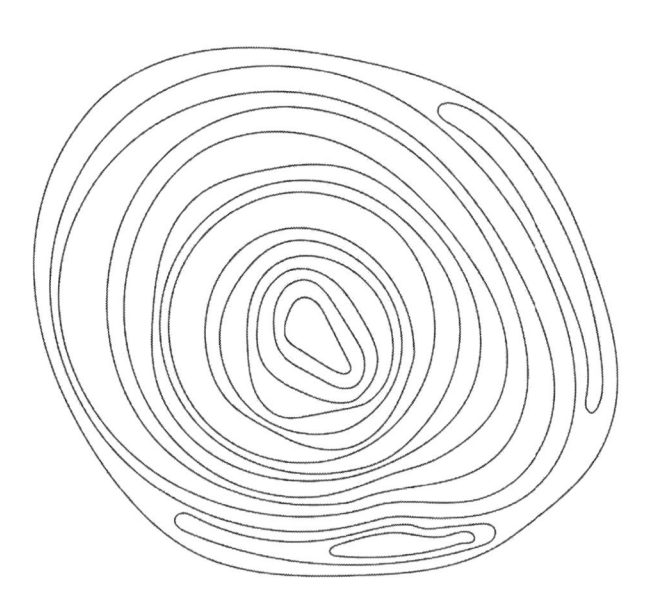

12.

YOU WILL HAVE TO MAKE SACRIFICES

Life is a game of trade. You'll have to make tough choices as to what you're going to give up at certain points in your life, because there will be times in your life when you can't have it all at the same time. I hate saying that. But know that you can always have and do great things.

13.

YOU CAN'T DO WHAT YOU WANT TO ALONE

If I've seen a little further or achieved a little more, it is because I've followed the trail of success and stood on the shoulders of giants. I know that in the world we live in, it's not what you know or even who you know that matters. Instead, it's all about who you know knows. To reach your potential you need access to an A Team, a posse, mentors, sponsors, coaches, counsellors, good friends, and networks. So, make sure to network and build relationships for they will return dividends. It's why people say your network is your net worth and why we work so hard on this at The Source.[1]

---

1. https://bit.ly/TheSourceWaitlist

Bet on you.
Invest in you.
When you do, others will.

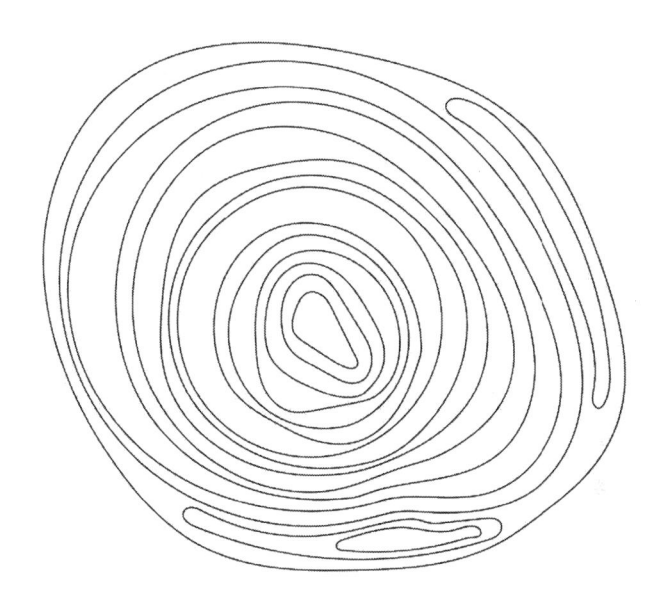

14.

WORK SMARTER, NOT HARDER

Success is a team sport; you need a strong team of people around you to keep you strong. Sometimes you'll need an introduction, a referral or recommendation. Other times you'll need a nudge, a push, a kind word or just to offload and be heard. Networking is an activity you must make time for, and it allows you to work smarter not harder. As different networks bring you different things, choose them carefully. Effective networking is not about how many people you know. That's just vanity. Rather, it's who those people are and the relationship you have with them, so always seek quality over quantity. Adopt a strategy where you identify and connect with people who are connected to multiple networks. This enables you to benefit from weak ties.[1] Make sure you include a strong inner circle of women, too. Research says that women are two and a half times more likely to be promoted when they have a strong circle of female friends at work.[2] So, instead of competing, form a circle of women around you and cheer for each other.

---

1. https://en.wikipedia.org/wiki/Interpersonal_ties
2. https://hbr.org/2019/02/research-men-and-women-need-different-kinds-of-networks-to-succeed

15.

FAIL FAST, FAIL FORWARD

There's no shame in failure. In fact, it's where your best learning lessons will originate. The more you fail the faster you'll succeed, so see setbacks as opportunities for personal expansion and spiritual growth. When you make a mistake, own up, apologise, and remember it. But don't accept it as proof that you're not capable of getting to where you want to be. Understand that your mind determines your direction, and your happiness depends on the quality of your thoughts. Many women deny themselves the power in failure. They believe in perfection instead, and that their failure is evidence that they are indeed an unworthy impostor. But failure should not invoke shame and output does not equal your worth. All failure is a learning lesson, and it shows you that you are progressing and that you're bringing your whole self to your career.

Some companies get this. They ask for your failure CV when hiring. They want to see what your risk appetite is like, how much you've learned, how well you adapt, and how resilient you are. Sara Blakely, the founder of Spanx (an intimate apparel company selling pants and leggings) is well known for telling the story of how her father made her recount her daily failures. He didn't punish her for her errors. Instead, he praised and encouraged her. And when it comes to women, the world needs more of this. We need parents, teachers, and company leaders to stretch and support us in equal doses. To instill psychological safety and not make women responsible for taking risks, telling them to take more and get used to this. It's about making women feel safer. Only then will we see the change everyone wants.

Only when women feel safer will we see the change everyone wants.

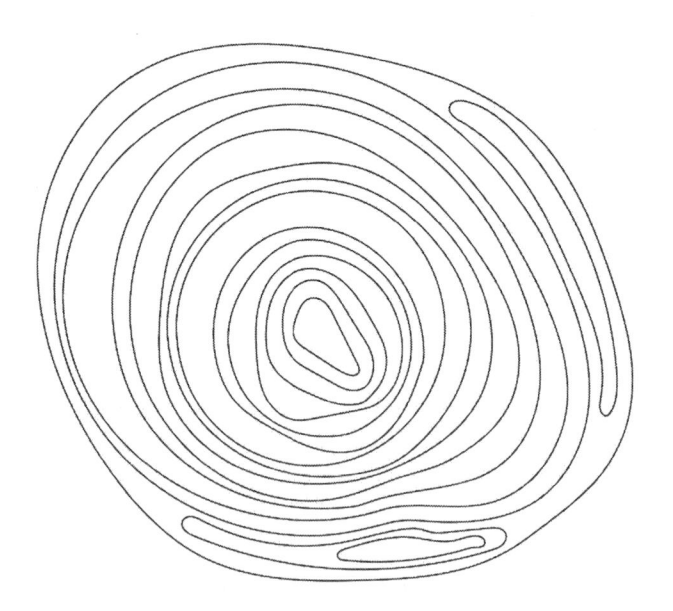

16.

YOU ARE HERE TO CHANGE THE GAME

You are not lacking. You are not limited. You've just been conditioned, along with many others to think that you're worthless, powerless and should beg for favour. This is not so. This is not your truth. You are complete. You are here to change the game, and it starts within you every single day. You are a mighty creation and capable of co-creation with life itself. That's how beloved you are, and you do not need to do anything to win favour. You are perfect. So, be true to yourself. Act with faith and speed but not like a high-achieving adrenaline junkie, which is so easy to do in male dominated professions like cybersecurity. Have courage to take steady steps forward, to get off the hamster wheel of life, and to ask for help if you don't know how.

17.

ASK DIRECTLY AND WITH A DECISION TIMESCALE

Asking for help isn't easy especially when you're keen to show your expertise, competence, and confidence. This is normal. Research in neuroscience and psychology explain that the social threats involved—uncertainty, risk of rejection, potential for diminished status, and inherent relinquishing of autonomy actually activate the same brain regions that physical pain does.[1]

To increase the likelihood of getting what you want, cut to the chase, and ask for what you want directly. Prior to having this conversation, build your case and have factual evidence ready, hold data driven

---

1. https://hbr.org/2018/05/how-to-get-the-help-you-need

conversations, and make sure you focus on what will add value to the person you're asking. Role play with someone as this can help. Try begging for what you want and asking for it as if you are a queen. Both are extremes and will probably make you laugh but importantly they'll also help you get into a more authentic and focused state. When you ask, pay attention to your body language. Hold a tall stance even if you're sitting. This aligns your energy and signals confidence. Show gratitude for where you are now but make sure you always approach your ask with the intention of receiving what you want. Literally, feel yourself having received what you want before asking for it. Think about the first steps you'd make having received what you desire. Get into that energy. If the person you're asking needs more time to consider what you want, make sure you get a timescale for a decision after. If you don't get what you ask for, try to understand why, and don't be hard on yourself. Acknowledge you've made a leap forward in terms of your self-development. And if you're still wondering whether you should ask for what you want or not, consider this: You'll never know unless you ask. You have nothing to lose but everything to gain.

Finally, understand that as a woman, you may be more comfortable in your role as a giver, due to the way you've been raised. So, know to leave your hands open when giving, as this is how reciprocity works. When your hands are open to giving, they are open to receive.

And if you're not asking, know that this can often reveal your independent side and a new conditioning for women. Typically, the independent woman can get what she wants but only if she's not seen to be needy. She rebels against the "good girl" stereotype who behaves, is modest, considerate, selfless, wants for nothing, and is content in a supportive, largely invisible role. So, watch out for her. You may encounter her most of the time or when triggered by certain people, relationships, or circumstances. If you recognise her, chances are you'll be feeling tired, a tad resentful and ready for change. And that's why it's time to ask for support, to knowingly work in a different manner, and to upgrade without shame or blame.

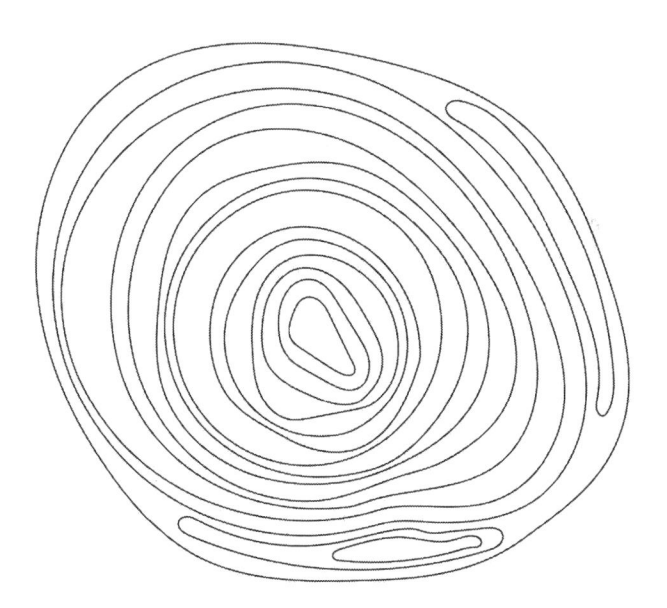

Focus on what and why.
Surrender how,
who and when.
Give thanks.
Be ready for miracles.

18.

GET OUT OF YOUR HEAD

You work in a knowledge driven industry and that means you're in your head a great deal of the time. Whilst your mind holds the key to your performance and is powerful beyond belief, don't forget your body. Unlike your mind, it won't trick you. It won't tell you everything's OK when everything isn't and you're on the edge of burnout. It's actually wiser, as it's where your intuition lies. Like most things in life, you need union, so your mind and body need to work together. So, even though you may feel tired, bogged down and that you need more sleep, check that it's not your soul that's tired. Chances are, it's yearning for adventure, freedom, nature, magic and stillness rather than more sleep. Let your feet touch the earth. Place your hands in the soil. Swim in the lake, river or ocean. Move. Walk. Dance. Sing. Be a wild woman – a free spirit. Shake off your day. Drain the heavy energy away when you wash. Awaken your soul, get into your body, free your mind. Tune into your feminine. Embrace the stillness, the quiet. You don't need to push and power through all the time.

19.

STOP TRYING TO BEAT THE PATRIARCHY

The only way you can beat the patriarchy is to stop trying to beat the patriarchy. It's about believing the rules of the game in business for women are different to those of men and are yet to be set. It's about not using the patriarchy as a benchmark. Instead of focusing on what *not* to be, it's about making the system irrelevant by creating a leap in value for buyers and partners. It's about collaboration, using data and smart thinking rather than force, fear and opposition. The world needs more companies to ensure their teams feel safe about taking more measured risks.

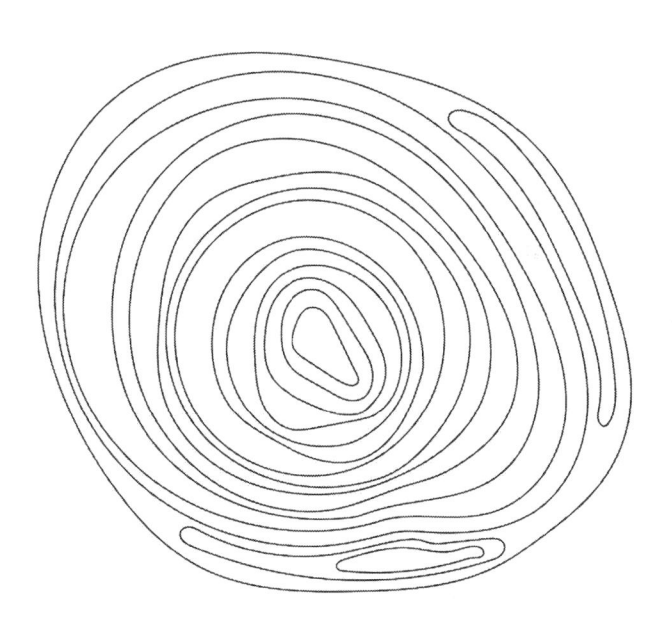

Time is just a statement of priority.
Get clear.
Make time.

20.

MIND THE COMPANY YOU KEEP

Stay away from anyone who demeans you or your ambitions. Insecure people always do that. Surround yourself with people who believe in you. People who will lift you higher and know what they're talking about. By all means listen to friends, peers, family and so on, but pay more attention to someone who has already done what you want to do. Their advice carries more weight than others. Also, never bad mouth anyone. It doesn't reflect well on you.

21.

YOUR MIND IS A TREASURE TROVE SO GUARD IT

Your mind is a treasure trove and container of power so hold the vision and it will open the gateway to the actualisations of your desire. If you can dream it, you can do it, but only if you focus, feel into the energy and act. If you fail to do this, it will remain a fantasy.

Be a wild woman – a free spirit.

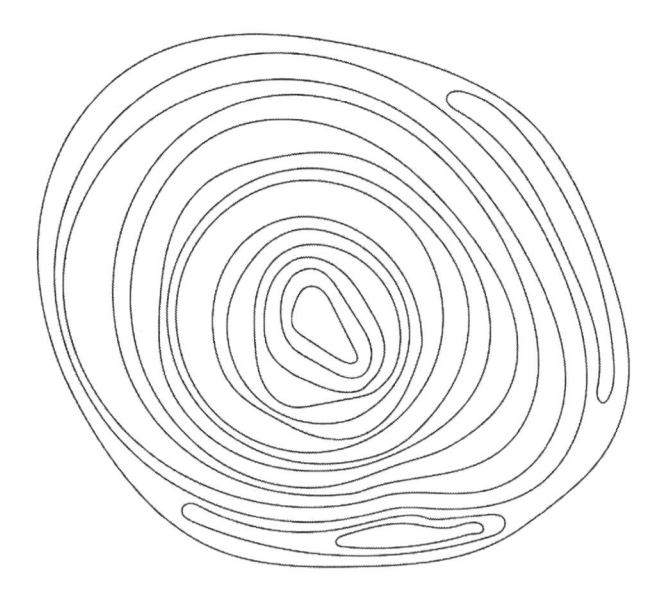

22.

DO ONE THING WELL AND BE KNOWN FOR IT

Take time to self-discover. Learn what you love and excel at. Get clarity on who you want to serve and what they seek. Create value for the right people to seek out and show integrity by doing what you say you're going to do.

23.

NOTHING LASTS FOREVER

No one thing or feeling is permanent. As night becomes day, so happiness and sadness replace one another. Accept each moment and know that whatever you're facing now will pass. It's nature's way and how life works.

24.

THE WORLD IS YOUR OYSTER

Understand your outer world is but a reflection of your inner world. Never has there been a more favourable time in history for you to excel than now. So, do the inner work you need to do and find a way to be unstoppable. Commit to making your desires happen. The barriers you believe to exist are false. The world is your oyster!

Activity brings clarity.
Take action.
There are **no wrong turns**.

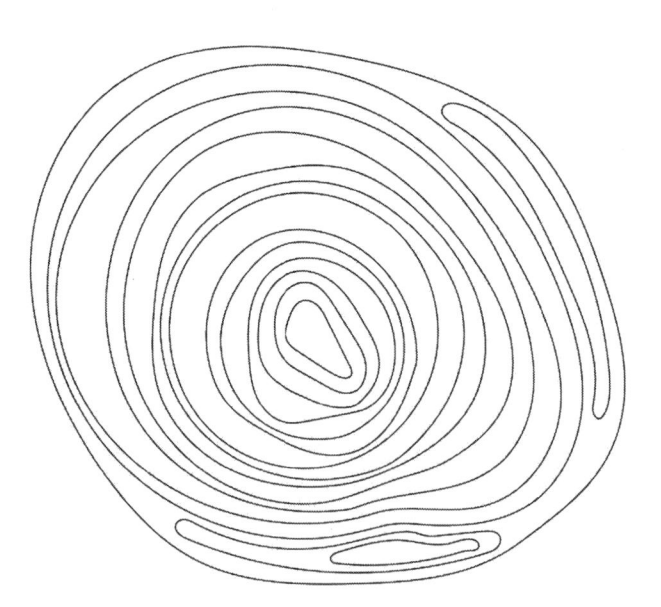

25.

COMPARISON IS THE THIEF OF JOY

These days everyone lives their life through a filter, on social media. Nobody's life is perfect and even when it appears to be, it never is. So, don't compare yourself to anyone else. It depletes you. Don't liken yourself to 'you' either. You are not the same person you were a year, month, week, day and second ago. Avoid judgment whenever you can. All too often as women, we're pitted against one another and divided. We compete fiercely for what's been limited to us – that promotion, project, award or recognition – and competition is wired into our DNA. So rather than adhering to the system and being weakened through a divide and conquer approach, protest with your behaviour. Don't judge, bad mouth or be disrespectful. There's no need to rescue anyone, either. Instead, when it comes to other women, do this: Lift them up. Amplify their voices. Credit them. Champion them and celebrate their successes as if they were your own. We are one.

26.

YOU ARE POWER

You don't need to reclaim your power. You don't even need to step into it. You are power. You're a life force and powerful beyond belief. By tapping into your intuition, you have an opportunity to connect with the essence of your being, to adjust your trajectory when you stray off course and to soar above your challenges. So, know your power and what to do with it. Align yourself with your heart and effortlessly enjoy the flow of love, joy and prosperity.

27.

YOU ARE NOT YOUR PAST

You are living a blessed life and your past does not affect your future unless you choose for that to be so. What you become therefore depends on what you decide to focus on. This means determining what habits you're going to cultivate, what books you're going to read, what affirmations you're going to recite, what company you're going to keep, what things mean to you, and what you're going to do about them. It's all of those things that determine your future.

The door of the cage is open.
Step out.
Free yourself.

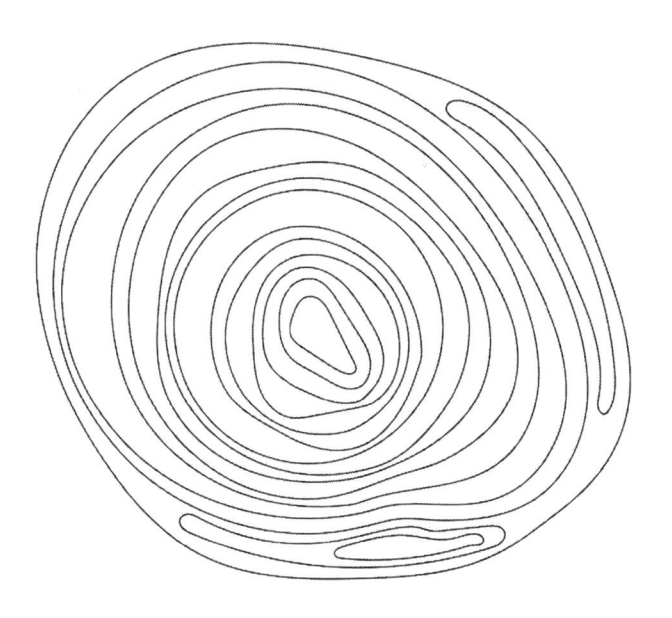

28.

STOP BUYING INTO THE PATRIARCHY'S PROPAGANDA

Banish the use of shared metaphors like *knocking on the door, crossing the firewall, navigating the labyrinth, smashing the glass ceiling,* and so on. Phrases like these undermine women[1], as they imply women have to break down barriers or alternatively take something that doesn't belong to them – something that they're not quite naturally entitled to.

Women are continually blamed for the male industry's lack of gender diversity. Often, we're told women don't apply for jobs because they don't like the work. But research suggests there are other reasons.

---

1. https://www.bbc.com/future/article/20170718-the-metaphors-that-shape-womens-lives

We're also told women need to be more confident, find their voices, reclaim their power and that we have to "see it to be it."

These phrases are ridiculous. Confidence is just about assessing risk and taking action on it so when the workplace becomes safer, women's actions will change. Women have a voice, let's set the record straight right now. It's never been lost. However, women may need help in using their voice or amplifying it so their message gets heard and is more impactful. As for power, all human beings are power, so a woman's power has never disappeared. But she may need help leveling up and avoiding workplace discrimination, so she reaches her potential. Finally, women don't need to see another woman doing a job in order to do it. We're not simpletons. Women can do anything they set their minds to do!

60 | STOP BUYING INTO THE PATRIARCHY'S PROPAGANDA

We are one.

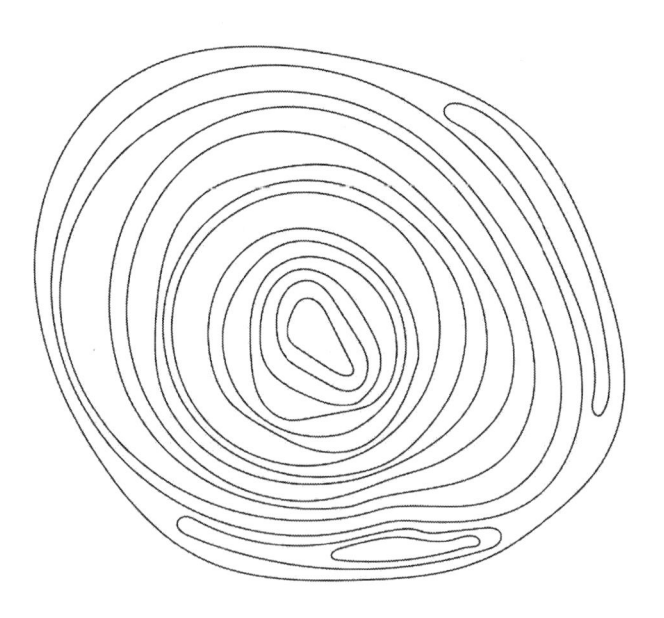

29.

PRACTICE OPPOSITION THINKING

The mind can only hold one thought at a time[1] and as women are so often bombarded by the patriarch's propaganda, when a negative thought comes up, take swift action and replace it with a positive one. This is you exercising control over your mind. Get it working on your terms – with you as the driver and not the drifter.

---

1. https://thepowermoves.com/brian-tracy/

30.

CULTIVATE AND EXUDE CERTAINTY

Whatever you believe to be true is constantly being reflected. It works like a mirror. If you believe you're unworthy, you'll constantly see that reflected and you'll see people treating you like that, too. If you believe people will only pay a certain price for your work, then that's the price you'll get. If you believe it's the end of your business and no one will commission any more work from you, then that's how it will be. If you're selling something – a product, service, initiative, concept, or yourself – don't just sell the features and benefits. Sell certainty. So, take this knowledge and use it. Cultivate and exude certainty, for when you change your beliefs and the way you look at things, the things you look at change, and most likely will shift in the right direction.

31.

BE FLEXIBLE; BEND LIKE THE REED

When it comes to your goals, dreams or even a decision you've made, adapt a *'bend but don't break'* approach. Perhaps you know the Aesop's Fable, where an oak and a reed were arguing about their strength. When a strong wind came up, the reed avoided being uprooted by bending and leaning with the gusts of wind. But the oak stood firm and was torn up by the roots. The fable deals with the contrasting behaviour of the oak, which trusts in its strength to withstand the storm and is blown over, and the reed that 'bends with the wind' survives. The moral of the fable is this: If you encounter obstacles along the way, don't quit and give up. Stay committed to your decision but be flexible with your approach. Once you've decided what you want, don't get stuck on the means to achieving it. Be resourceful. Stay open, attentive, and flexible.

Progress not perfection.
Skills are built not inbuilt.

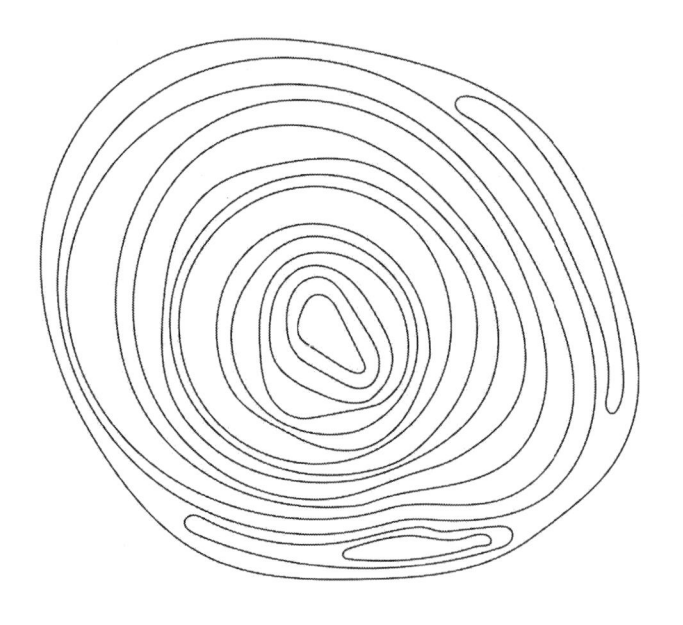

32.

BUILD STRENGTH BY RECOUNTING YOUR SUCCESSES

Life is a roller coaster. Sometimes you're slowly making your way up and other times you're shooting down, fast. Success on the other hand is a habit so when you're feeling low, rejected or bypassed, which will happen at some points in your life and career, recount your successes. Start from your earliest memory. Write them down in a book using pen and paper so you can refer to them whenever you need to. Don't do this on a device. You need to feel the energy flowing through your body and into the pen and onto the paper.

33.

REGRESSION IS NOT ALWAYS A WORSENING

Creation isn't linear, nor is learning. If you've ever taught or noticed how you've learned, you'll know this. Sometimes you have to go backwards and regress in order to move forward. If this happens prepare to advance fast. See the archer who draws back her bow and know that you are her arrow who'll be shot forward.

34.

WOMAN PLANS, GOD LAUGHS

We all know the saying *'Man plans, God laughs'* but the same is true for women. God (or life) has a sense of humour, and it's going to laugh at you throughout your life especially when you make a plan. Don't let it stop you. You need a plan for the magic (of life) to happen. Pay attention and enjoy the humour.

Women can do anything they set their minds to do!

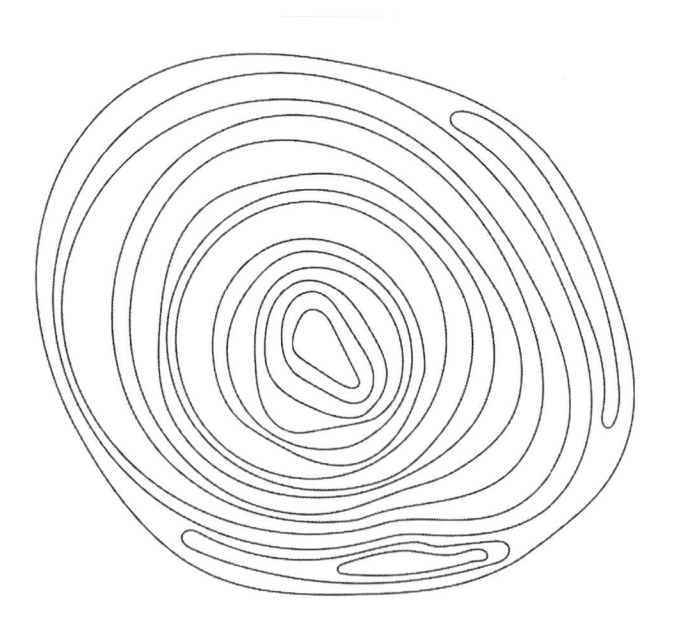

35.

LEAN BACK AS WELL AS IN

Recently, thanks to Sheryl Sandberg, many women have been conditioned to lean in, but the thing is you actually need to lean back at certain times too. When planning, if you lean forward to your dreams, too much, you'll only get stressed, will repel what you desire, and life or work will become an uphill struggle.

The reason why is because attracting what you want doesn't come from attachment to it. Rather, it comes from letting go, allowing and expanding. You see, when you dare to dream and set an intention, you must lean back and let go of how it comes to fruition. Letting go of your attachment is letting go of control and needing to control comes from not trusting the process. Attachment creates resistance, dependence and friction. But by leaning back and letting go, you allow everything to happen in a way that your ego can't even dream of. You free yourself from any burden or pressure. And of course, to free up your own desire is to become the woman who can have it.

36.

SURRENDER AND FREE UP DESIRE

When it feels like you're pushing a boulder uphill or paddling upstream, pay attention, for this often signals that things aren't aligned and it's time to 'course correct' your efforts. When things are meant to be, they flow with ease and grace. Doors open. The right people who can help you appear. The money you need lands. Nothing feels hard and that's when miracles, magic and serendipity happens.

You have to put in the effort and do the work, though. You also have to expand your thinking because at times you'll have to jump and know that you'll get wings or that a net will appear to catch you. And this is hard because most of the time as women we've been conditioned to fear this kind of mental expansion as it feels unsafe, and requires the power duo – faith and courage, which are often harder to access than ready-made how-to-books, step-by-step checklists, and training programs.

37.

GET GOOD AT MAKING DECISIONS

When you get stuck on a decision, it's easy to avoid taking action and to procrastinate. Unless you're in a trough – which is when you won't be thinking clearly – assess the risk you're feeling because that's what's going on, and then do this. Think of someone you admire and ask what advice they would give you. This helps you detach and think more clearly. It will also empower you as you learn to rely on yourself. Of course, you can ask for help and seek guidance from others, but don't absolve yourself of this responsibility. By handing over your decision making, you are weakening.

If you're unsure of your career direction and are concerned about what decision to make, ask yourself this: What if there were no wrong decisions, wrong turns, or mistakes? What if every decision you made would lead you to success? What would you do? Then, thinking about this, take a small step forward. After that, take another step. Keep doing this as this is you breaking things down and making things less overwhelming. It's you removing a lie that we've all been fed – that we need to know where we're going, what we're doing and maybe even what our purpose in life is. But often we don't, and it's only activity that brings us the clarity we need in order to discover what it is that we want.

If you don't ask, you don't get. Build your case. Ask clearly.

38.

NO MORE TRASH TALK

These day's it's hard to escape gender diversity targets and some companies are pushing them more than others. Targets are needed because what gets measured improves. However, if you've been recruited into a company, firm or institution that's pushing them, don't believe that you're only there to satisfy a target. You're there because of your ability. No company would waste their money on someone who couldn't add value and perform in accordance with their needs. Whilst they may choose you over a man, seize this opportunity. Grab it with both arms. Get over your pride. Don't let your ego get in the way and bring you down. And NEVER doubt your ability. Don't subject yourself to this trash talk. It's abusive. Build your strength. Work on your belief. See your value. Guard your mind.

39.

WILL IT AND WORK IT

As a woman in a male dominated industry, you're breaking boundaries, disrupting the status quo and having to deal with obstacles and challenges, like negativity and rejection all the time. It can be exhausting. Developing the right mindset is the key to propel yourself forward in your own journey to success. You must adopt a growth mindset[1] and stay open rather than fixed or closed. Successful women do this. They rise to challenges, set boundaries and understand that some opportunities aren't really opportunities at all. Instead, they're there to distract them. Importantly, though, they use their intuition, ambition, inner drive, experience and network to keep

---

1. https://en.wikipedia.org/wiki/Carol_Dweck

them focused. In order to get to where you want you have to set an intention – will it – and take action – work it.

40.

IF YOU WANT TO DO MORE, DO LESS

When Gandhi had a tough day ahead of him, he mediated for two-hours not one. As counter intuitive as it might appear, in order to do more, you have to do less. There's been loads of research into this. Parkinson's law also says that work expands to fill the time available for its completion. As women we do a lot and it's easy to feel overburdened or burned out. So, if you're struggling to get something done in your day and you can't delegate it or get help, take a break. Walk, do some other form of exercise, mediate, tap, or clear some space and declutter. You'll find your mind will be clearer, you'll be more energised, and you'll work faster.

Visibility equals credibility. Get out there. Evidence output.

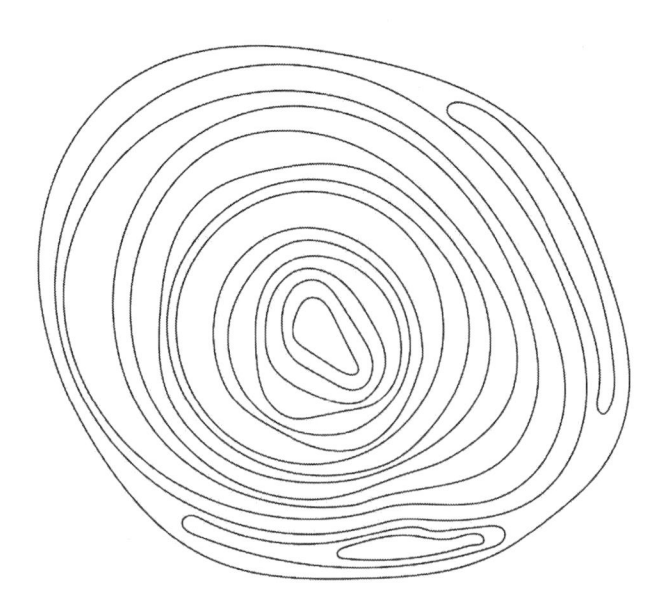

41.

FOCUS ON THINGS WITHIN YOUR CONTROL

There may be times that you feel discriminated against, unheard, undervalued and not treated fairly but don't waste your time pointing fingers and playing the blame game. You are not a victim so don't act like one. Although you may, or may not, have an impact on what someone else is thinking, feeling or doing you have a choice about the beliefs you hold and how you react. So, don't sell yourself short or sell yourself out. As I've said before, you get what you're willing to tolerate and that's why it's best not to put up or look the other way. That way, things just continue. Voice your opinion, stand firm in your convictions and take action. Do the right rather than easiest thing.

42.

GROW INTO FORGIVENESS AND LET GO OF EMOTIONAL HURTS

Bad feelings and hate can fester and destroy you. Don't let this happen. When you forgive others, you create a bridge of forgiveness to yourself and an essential path to your freedom. Forgiveness helps you understand and heal the experiences in your life that you've attracted, participated in, or have been affected by. It's a gift to yourself, and whilst it can't change the past, it can and will change your future. When you feel too weak to forgive and find yourself harbouring festering hurts and developing a 'poor me' complex or victim mentality, then it's time to work on yourself.

One way to do this is to write. As you write down your hurt, you'll notice something really interesting happening – the experiences and emotional hurts that are troubling you will move from your subconscious mind to your conscious mind as you relive them. This emotion comes out of the experience and flows through your body. If you're writing on a notepad it will go down your hand and onto the paper. To rid yourself of the energy, all you need to do is crumple the piece of paper and burn it. And, depending on the intensity of the emotion, you may need to write about it several times. Now, the fire won't destroy the emotion because you can't destroy energy. But what you can do is transfer and transform the emotion that's inside of you into another matter.

Note, we accept no liability for any fires you cause. Please be responsible!

Build your strength.
Work on your belief.
See your value.
Guard your mind.

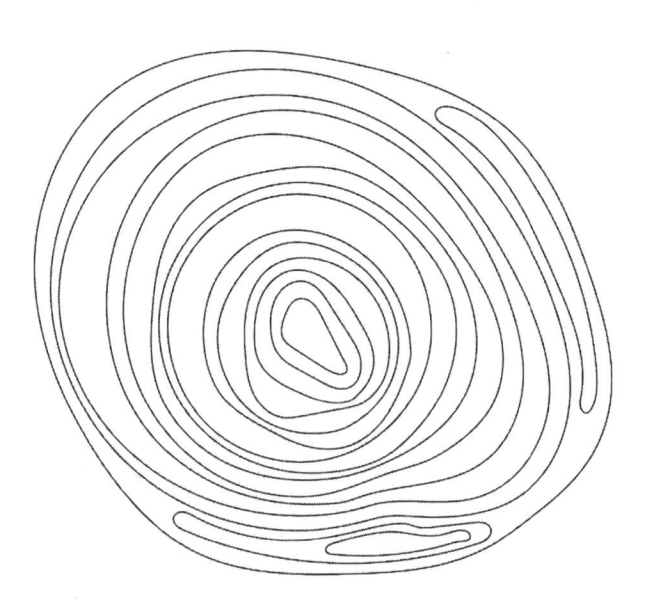

43.

YOU HAVE A VOICE SO USE IT

In male dominated industries, women are regularly interrupted, spoken over, and have their ideas stolen by men. It's frustrating, irritating and you mustn't let it continue. To stop it, you don't have to adopt a rude behaviour and mirror them, but you do have to be assertive, claim what's yours, speak with conviction, certainty and insist on having your say.

If you're not being heard, try talking more loudly, lowering your pitch, keeping it even, and ensuring you end sentences with a lower inflection. The reason for this latter recommendation is because men hear differently than women. It turns out that women's voices affect a man's brain differently, so they have more trouble hearing female voices especially as they age. A study at the University of Sheffield discovered that whilst both men and women process voice sound in Wernicke's area, in the left cerebral hemisphere, men only tend to process male voice sounds there.[1] They save female voice sounds for the auditory portion of the right hemisphere, which is where they process melody lines or background music. As women listen with both hemispheres, they're able to pick up more nuances of sound and voice tonality, for example, crying or warning tones. But, as men listen with one hemisphere primarily, they're less able.

---

1. http://arlenetaylor.org/sensory-preference-pas/7444-gender-hearing-differences

44.

DON'T WAIT FOR PERMISSION

If you're good at your job, it's highly likely you'll be offered the opportunity to lead a project, team or initiative. Don't turn this down but don't wait for this to happen either. Look for unassigned projects or problems that need solving in your workplace and push yourself forward to be the person who'll take charge and resolve them. If you're not allowed to, don't become bitter and don't let this derail you from your career goal. Ask for feedback, adapt, and keep going for what you want. If you can't get it and this keeps on happening, consider changing jobs or doing things your own way as an entrepreneur. That way you'll be able to create your own rules and be free to chart your path.

You are worthy.
Full stop.
Your worth is not
measured by your output.

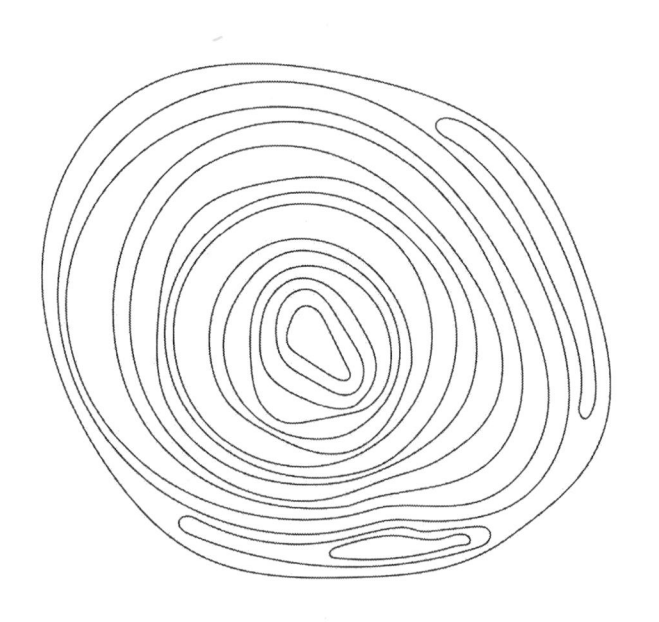

45.

BE GRATEFUL AND AMBITIOUS

You are living a blessed life and what blesses you, blesses everyone. Give thanks for this. Nothing generates good will or builds trust and morale among those you work and interact with more powerfully than a gracious attitude. Let your thoughts linger on your achievements and your future ambitions. Say thank you more – to your team, friends, family, supporters, and yourself. With your ambition, you raise your expectations and energy but be aware of gratitude's limitations. Whilst it has many benefits it's also what keeps women confined and the gender gap, particularly pay and promotion, expanding. The entitlement and collusion of men plays a part too. However, the gratitude of women enslaves us. The patriarchy exploits this and survives by using the tokenism of a few women to maintain control over the rest of us. Working in a male dominated industry, with many organisations being targeted on gender diversity, it's time to exploit this. So, be brave. Expect more. Demand more.

46.

NO ONE RULE FITS FOR WOMEN WHO APOLOGISE

For many, apologies have become our de-facto way of communicating, and there's always a place for them. However, when they become a habit and are overused by women, we're told they can sabotage our authority and damage our career. But what we're not told – unless we're speaking to a linguist – is that saying sorry is actually a ritual way of restoring balance to a conversation and that language is highly contextual in nature. So, women who say sorry are not wrong and shouldn't be shamed for apologising. Communicating at work is complex and women are still in a double bind due to stereotypes. What matters, therefore, is that you test and pay attention to what works for you. Know that using the same techniques as men can backfire because you're already fighting against so many cultural assumptions. So, what you may notice is that in many instances you'll be more respected and successful when you conform to gendered expectations.

Voice your opinion, stand firm in your convictions and take action.

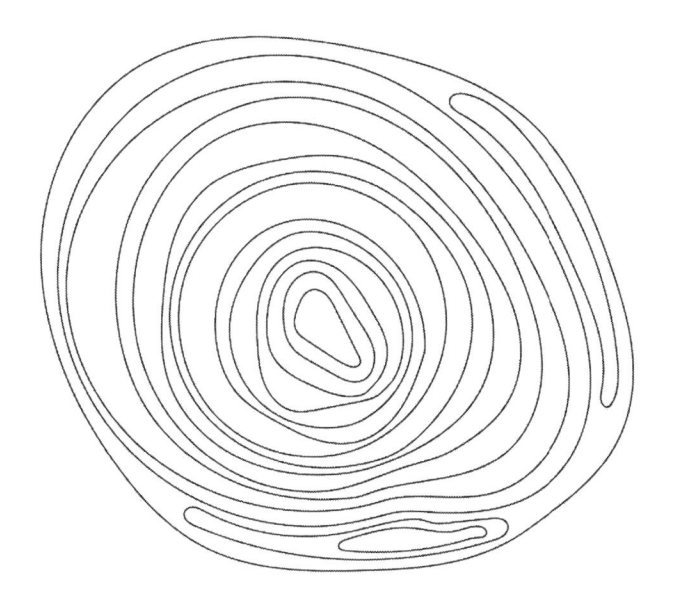

47.

PICK YOUR BATTLES AND HANDLE CONFLICT WELL

Sometimes the easiest thing to do is to wage war on someone or some organisation especially if it's in the name of women's rights. Whilst I advocate standing your ground and seeking equality, I encourage you to pick your battles wisely. Sometimes this means letting things go and conserving your energy. Other times it means standing up for what you know to be right. So, choose what's important to you and ask yourself, *'Will it help or hurt?'* Whatever you decide, know this: All genders are not the same and that's a good thing. So, celebrate this; be appreciative and respectful. We must come together but be allowed to separate and find our own groups without fear.

When it comes to conflict, neither seek it nor avoid it. When it occurs, be forward-looking and positive.

Don't attack anyone personally, don't let them attack you, and if you can, calm down before doing anything. When dealing with conflict, you can say things like, *"I hear you,"* and *"help me understand,"* but you must ask, *"how do we move past this?"* Stay focused on the issue at hand. Be open and deal with conflict face-to-face. If you can't and you're conversing in an email, text or message, document what you need and be very careful not to read emotion or tone into it when it's not there. Hold positive regard, exercise your ability to constructively voice your view and stand firm. As Ruth Bader Ginsburg said, *"Fight for the things you care about but do so in a way that leads others to join you."*

48.

DON'T BECOME ATTACHED, HAVE A PLAN B

When you become attached to something or someone you become dependent and controllable. This makes you weak, keeps you trapped and unfree. Spread your risk and have a Plan B. This doesn't mean you can't be committed. It means you can be more so. When you have a Plan B, this is like having brakes on a car. They were made so that the car could go faster. Now think about how you'll feel and what you'll do when you get blindsided because the promotion you've earned has been given to your male counterpart. Plan Bs change the power dynamic. They are empowering.

How you do anything is how you do everything.
Pick your standards.
Be known for them.

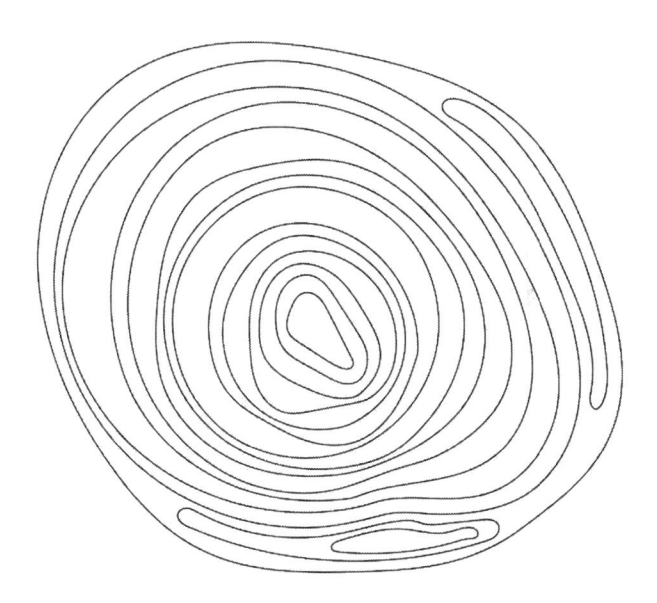

49.

SAY NO MORE OFTEN

At different points in your career, you may need to say yes more often than no, especially to activities that will take you out of your comfort zone. However, when you say yes to something it takes you away from other activities. This could be time with your friends, loved ones and family. Or this could be a piece of work you want or need to do. So, consider carefully what you say yes and no to. People will put you on the spot, but you can always say you need time to consider and return to them with an answer.

When you want to get more done, you're going to need to focus. That means guarding your time and saying no more often. When it comes to missed opportunities, don't concern yourself with them by buying into a scarcity mindset. People will manipulate you all the time with this trick. If you buy into an abundant mindset, know that opportunities are still going to be there for you and if things are meant to be, they'll be. Nothing that's meant for you will surpass you. So, practice saying no. Role play it with a friend. Notice how you feel and what resistance shows up in your body. Chances are it will as your "good girl" upbringing will want you to oblige, harmonise, people please and maintain the status quo. Finally, if you're a parent, teach your daughter/s to say no. Get them to stand in front of the mirror saying it often or you try it with them.

You are power.
You are enough.
You've got this.

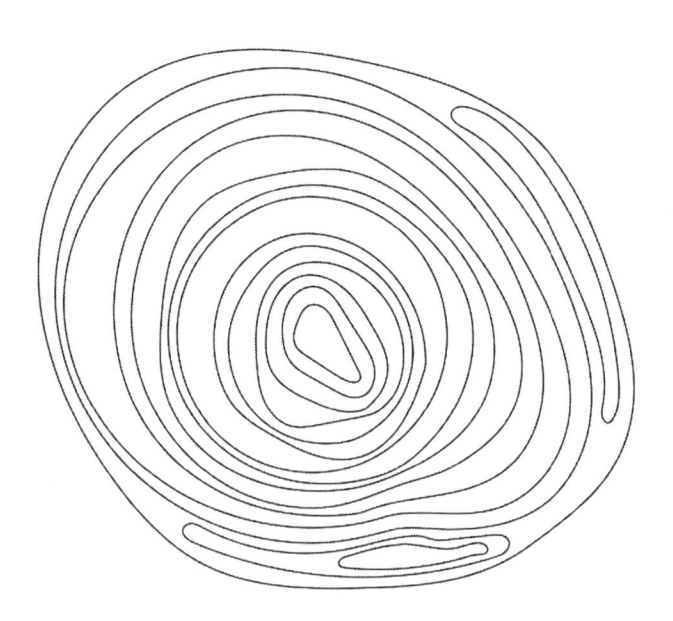

50.

TIME IS JUST A STATEMENT OF PRIORITY

Time is just a statement of priority and when you use it as a reason for not doing something, you hold yourself back. As we all have 24-hours in our day, what you're doing when you use time as a reason for not taking action on something is letting others know your priorities, what matters to you, and where you are with your activities. You're also triggering scarcity in your brain rather than abundance, which is limiting. When you stop affirming a lack of time, you'll stop experiencing a lack of time.

When you become a source of time, you can create more time. It sounds impossible but when you go more slowly, you'll find you'll speed up. That's why there's a saying: "less haste more speed." So, before using time as a reason for not doing something, take a critical look at what's going on. Examine your priorities and time management. Check you're not taking on too many tasks and let your manager know if they're overloading you. Whether you think you have enough time or not, you're right.

51.

USE MASCULINE AND FEMININE ENERGIES

Typically, as women we prickle when certain qualities are labelled as being inherently masculine (e.g., assertive, dominant, rational, ambitious, independent, logical, headstrong, etc.) or feminine (e.g., intuitive, sensitive, modest, humble, nurturing, caring, compassionate, intuitive, heart strong, etc.). But women who advance in their careers and achieve the level of success they're capable of understand that these polarities must be worked in the workplace and that they're not actually attached to any one gender.

Most women understand the power of reciprocation, too, and that you get what you give. However, not as many understand the powerful masculine and feminine energies of giving and receiving. But if you've studied Eastern philosophy, you'll know about yinyang, and that giving is a masculine action (yang) and receiving is a feminine action (yin). Additionally, that all human beings contain both energies and feelings of congruence and fulfilment can only come about when these two energies are working in harmony.

As women, this doesn't mean you have to take on a persona and become something you're not, but it does mean using these energies strategically and for your own well-being. This can be hard in a male dominated workplace as receiving help is a much more vulnerable action than giving. Author and vulnerability expert Dr. Brené Brown says it's *"because you can stay armoured up and give, but you cannot stay armoured up and receive."* And many women are used to donning their armour as they battle in the workplace. As a minority set and outlier, it can often be hard for women to receive and not to judge themselves and others too harshly when help is offered. So, if you recognise this within yourself, deal with this by becoming aware of what's going on and commit to developing yourself into becoming the woman you need to be in order to create what you want. Have an accountability system (e.g., a coach, mentor, accountability buddy, good friend, family member or online system) in place, too, as this will increase your chances of success.

52.

CARE ABOUT BEING RESPECTED MORE THAN BEING LIKED

As a woman in a male dominated industry, you're going to face discrimination daily, and chances are you'll feel like you can't win either. Being continually judged, you face a trade-off between being liked or being respected. If you conform to the feminine stereotype of being nurturing and caring, you run the risk of being regarded as likeable, but not competent – which is code for technical. The same is true for women who appease others. They're more likely to be trampled on rather than appreciated. This response is standard for male dominated professions, and even with great many male supporters, when you're hired, developed, compensated and promoted it's likely you'll face criticism. It's grossly unfair. Yet, repeatedly because of the biases each of us hold, people tend to respond to successful, confident women much like they do to immoral men – they don't like them, and don't want to work with them.

To handle this bind, you have several choices. For example, you can modify your approach to find out what works for you. This will mean becoming highly attuned to those you're communicating with, drawing on your social intelligence, and continually adapting your style for each person. You can decide upon your communication and leadership style, be content operating in the fixed manner you choose, and deal with the judgement. Alternatively, you can become an entrepreneur. Putting aside the challenges associated with women raising funds, I've found much less discrimination.

108 | CARE ABOUT BEING RESPECTED MORE THAN BEING LIKED

**No more tolerating.
Be brave.
Expect more.
Demand more.**

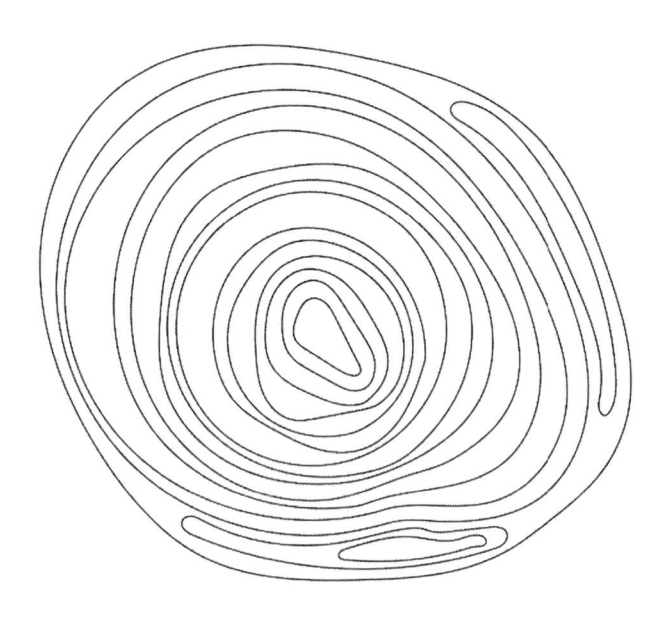

FINAL INSIGHT...

Our planet is suffering. The world is volatile and in a state of disarray. Right now, we have incredibly complex issues to solve. In cybersecurity, national, international, and online threats are becoming progressively integrated as adversaries develop new means to exploit vulnerabilities across borders and between cyber and physical worlds. And here's the truth bomb many discount: the typical cybersecurity set-up is unsuccessful in predicting, detecting, blocking, or effectively remediating cyberattacks.

Women can transform this. History has proved this time and time again, for when at war, leaders call on women. Thankfully, organisations are waking up to this and that's why we as women, must play a better game in business. Now is the time for us to take responsibility for our own success. So, use the insights contained within this book to power up, learn new ways of being, and design a career and life plan that meets your needs. You can't leave this to anyone else. You have to transform. To evolve. Not because you are wrong, but just because right now doing this enables us to break a dysfunctional system, the patriarchy. As women we can make things right for all people. We are natural change agents and guardians. You owe it to yourself, the future generations, and the planet to act now.

Think for one moment. How could you do this? What first step would you take to make it so? Would it be to share more of your insights with the women you love and respect? Would it be to come together to learn a new way of being in the workplace, a secret code? Would it be to hold each other accountable, to cheer each other on from the side-lines, to motivate, inspire, solve problems collectively, collaborate, co-create? Would it be to learn from trusted sources so you could stride confidently forward, clear on your pathway?

I believe it would, and that's why I want to ask you if you'd be willing to join me and other wonderful women at The Source, my brand-new platform for women in cyber, because that's where this is happening?

If the answer is yes, head over to https://bit.ly/TheSourceWaitlist

ABOUT JANE FRANKLAND

Jane Frankland is an award-winning leader, best-selling author, speaker, mother and women's change agent. Having spent over two decades in cybersecurity, Jane has become one of the most celebrated female influencers in the world and UNESCO has called her a trailblazing woman in tech. She built her own global hacking firm in the late 90s, has worked as an executive for world renown consultancies and contributed to leading industry accreditations, schemes and forums. She is a popular keynote speaker, university guest lecturer, awards judge and regularly shares her expertise in iconic media, including the top British broadsheets. She believes the world will only become safer, happier, and more prosperous with more women in male dominated industries and it's why today she works with women and businesses who value them through her latest initiative, The Source. There, she follows her passion to make women in cybersecurity standard not exception. You can find out more at https://jane-frankland.com

RESOURCES

Download 52 empowering quotes at
https://bit.ly/INSightsResources

Sign up for Jane's new books at
https://bit.ly/new-book-waitlist

Order Jane's new planner at
https://bit.ly/TheSourcePlanner

WORK WITH JANE

There are many ways to work with Jane depending on whether you are an individual or corporate client. As an individual woman, you've already been invited to join The Source. Please do it. I'd love to see you there. If you're a corporate client, here are some opportunities for you.

Book Jane to speak

There's a reason why Jane is known to attract an audience. It's because she delivers thought-provoking insights and actionable tools in regard to cybersecurity and women, coupled with passion and inspiration. Her audiences always return to their work charged, upbeat, more knowledgeable, and ready to face any challenge thrown at them.

Over the past few years, she's been engaged to speak at hundreds of events around the world for forward thinking companies, governments, societies, plus the United Nations, European Commission and India

High Commission. Additionally, for some of the world's largest events like WebSummit, Harvard Asia, Sibos and Black Hat. Although she can accommodate small groups, her audience sizes typically range from 100 to 2,000+. The topics she speaks mainly about are in the cybersecurity field and relate to the challenges businesses face in regard to protecting their assets, women, technology and entrepreneurship.

Book Jane to train

Jane has designed and developed tailored, targeted, and impactful programmes for women that have a sustained and positive impact on participants – and on their organisations. Her programmes are available for executive and emerging leaders, as well as for graduates and middle managers. Her flagship training programme, IN Demand 10X exists to amplify women's voices and create visible female role models. It covers personal branding, communication, networking, resilience, confidence, influence, and executive presence. It's designed to be fun, highly interactive, and inspiring by incorporating stories and real-life examples, the latest brain research and exercises.

Her leadership programmes equip organisations with a dynamic end-to-end process for developing leaders at all levels. They work by taking existing, popular models of management and combining them in a particular order – the order that research has shown successful leaders use them in – to give a blueprint for leading and developing high performance in organisations.

Book Jane to get more women into your team

Being able to get in front of women in cybersecurity, connect with them and lead them to your hiring opportunities is essential, and The Source platform can enable that.

The Source exists to help women and businesses who value them in cybersecurity. It's where we come together to add value, not point fingers. It's where we collaborate, unify, and create communities that are positive, accessible, and valuable. It's where we empower women to build their networks, grow their skills and access essential resources. And it's where we help forward- thinking businesses to draw on a rich, diverse pool of female talent.

The Source operates on a global basis and while most of our clients include some of the world's best-known brands, many of whom are listed on the global stock indices, we also have a selection of start-up and mid-range organisations. Our solutions incorporate consulting, training, mentoring, certification, and talent acquisition. They align to the 2030 United Nations Sustainable Development Goal 5, 10 and 16.

Take the next step

Book a discovery call with Jane and her team on: https://jane-frankland.com/contact

SPONSOR JANE'S WOMEN IN CYBERSECURITY PLATFORM, THE SOURCE

The Source exists to help women and businesses who value them in cybersecurity. It's where we come together to add value, not point fingers. It's where we collaborate, unify and create communities that are positive, accessible and valuable. It's where we empower women in cybersecurity to build their networks, grow their skills and access essential resources. And it's where we help forward- thinking businesses to draw on a rich, diverse pool of female talent.

The Source operates on a global basis and while most of our corporate clients include some of the world's best-known brands, many of whom are listed on the global stock indices, we also have a selection of start-up and mid-range organisations who are championing our mission. Our solutions include a unique platform and incorporate consulting, training, mentoring, certification and talent acquisition. The Source is a socially responsive organisation, with a women's foundation. Our work aligns to the 2030 United Nations Sustainable Development Goal 5, 10 and 16.

To find out more, visit the source.is or contact hello@thesource.is

OTHER BOOKS BY JANE FRANKLAND

To order volume copies of Jane's books for book signings, please email hello@jane-frankland.com

Printed in Great Britain
by Amazon